ABRAHAM LINCOLN
(1809–1865)

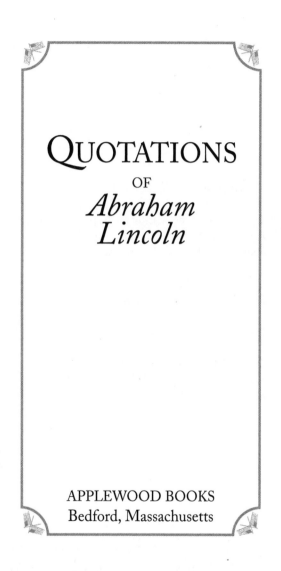

QUOTATIONS

OF

Abraham Lincoln

APPLEWOOD BOOKS
Bedford, Massachusetts

ISBN 978-1-55709-941-9

20 19 18 17 16 15 14 13 12 11

Manufactured in U.S.A.

Abraham Lincoln

ABRAHAM LINCOLN was born in a one-room log cabin in Kentucky on February 12, 1809. His family moved from Kentucky to the backwoods of Indiana when he was eight. When he was nine, his mother died. As a young man, Lincoln did not have much formal schooling, but when he wasn't plowing and planting, he was reading borrowed books and weekly newspapers.

Lincoln settled in New Salem, Illinois, where he worked and lived for a while in a general store. During this time he was honing his skills as a debater. When the Black Hawk War broke out in 1832, Lincoln enlisted and was chosen a captain. At the age of twenty-four, Lincoln was elected to the Illinois Legislature. At this time, he began studying law. In 1837, Lincoln moved to Springfield and began a career in law, first with John Stuart, later with Stephen Logan, and in 1844, he established the firm of Lincoln and Herndon.

In 1842, Lincoln married Mary Todd. They had four boys, Robert, Edward, William, and Thomas. In 1858, Lincoln ran against Stephen A. Douglas for Senator. He lost the election, but in debating with Douglas he gained a national reputation that won him the Republican nomination for President.

In November of 1860, Lincoln was elected the sixteenth President. Even before he was inaugurated in March of 1861, Lincoln's Presidency was marked by the secession of the southern states and Lincoln's duty-bound efforts to preserve the Union. It resulted in four years of bloody battle on American soil.

In 1864, Lincoln won reelection, as Union military triumphs heralded an end to the war. In his planning for peace, the President was flexible and generous, encouraging Southerners to lay down their arms and join speedily in reunion. His Second Inaugural Address, delivered March 5, 1865, promised victory for the North and assured charity to the South: "With malice toward none; with charity for all. . ."

On Good Friday, April 14, 1865, five days after Lee surrendered at Appomattox, with plans for reconstruction under way, Lincoln was assassinated at Ford's Theatre in Washington. He died the following day.

QUOTATIONS
OF
*Abraham
Lincoln*

*L*et us have faith that right makes might; and in that faith let us to the end dare to do our duty as we understand it.

A. Lincoln

*W*hy should there not be a patient confidence in the ultimate justice of the people? Is there any better or equal hope in the world?

A. Lincoln

I have stepped out upon this platform that I may see you and that you may see me, and in the arrangement I have the best of the bargain.

A. Lincoln

*N*ever let your correspondence fall behind.

*E*very blade of grass is a study; and to produce two, where there was but one, is both a profit and a pleasure.

A.Lincoln

*I*n this sad world of ours, sorrow comes to all; and, to the young, it comes with bitterest agony, because it takes them unawares.

A.Lincoln

I have found that when one is embarrassed, usually the shortest way to get through with it is to quit talking or thinking about it, and go at something else.

A.Lincoln

*L*eave nothing for tomorrow which can be done today.

*L*et me not be understood as saying that there are no bad laws, nor that grievances may not arise for the redress of which no legal provisions have been made. I mean to say no such thing. But I do mean to say that although bad laws, if they exist, should be repealed as soon as possible, still, while they continue in force, for the sake of example they should be religiously observed.

A.Lincoln

*W*ill springs from the two elements of moral sense and self-interest.

A.Lincoln

*L*et not him who is houseless pull down the house of another; but let him labor diligently and build one for himself, thus by example assuring that his own shall be safe from violence when built.

$\mathcal{T}$ruth is generally the best vindication against slander.

A. Lincoln

$\mathcal{I}$t is said an Eastern monarch once charged his wise men to invent him a sentence to be ever in view, and which should be true and appropriate in all times and situations. They presented him the words: "And this, too, shall pass away." How much it expresses! How chastening in the hour of pride! How consoling in the depths of affliction!

A. Lincoln

$\mathcal{I}$t is not merely for today, but for all time to come that we should perpetuate for our children's children this great and free government, which we have enjoyed all our lives.

Plainly, the central idea of secession, is the essence of anarchy.

A. Lincoln

I have never studied the art of paying compliments to women; but I must say that if all that has been said by orators and poets since the creation of the world in praise of woman were applied to the women of America, it would not do them justice for their conduct during this war. . . God bless the women of America!

A. Lincoln

Let every American, every lover of liberty, every well wisher to his posterity, swear by the blood of the Revolution, never to violate in the least particular, the laws of the country; and never to tolerate their violation by others.

I have endured a great deal of ridicule without much malice; and have received a great deal of kindness, not quite free from ridicule. I am used to it.

A. Lincoln

*T*hose who deny freedom to others, deserve it not for themselves.

A. Lincoln

*L*et reverence for the laws be breathed by every American mother to the lisping babe that prattles on her lap. Let it be taught in schools, in seminaries, and in colleges. Let it be written in primers, spelling books, and in almanacs. Let it be preached from the pulpit, proclaimed in legislative halls, and enforced in the courts of justice. And, in short, let it become the political religion of the nation.

When the conduct of men is designed to be influenced, persuasion, kind, unassuming persuasion, should ever be adopted.

A. Lincoln

Labor is prior to, and independent of, capital. Capital is only the fruit of labor, and could never have existed if labor had not first existed. Labor is the superior of capital, and deserves much the higher consideration.

A. Lincoln

My paramount object in this struggle is to save the Union, and is not either to save or to destroy slavery. If I could save the Union without freeing any slave I would do it, and if I could save it by freeing all the slaves I would do it; and if I could save it by freeing some and leaving others alone I would also do that.

Yield larger things to which you can show no more than equal right; and yield lesser ones, though clearly your own. Better give your path to a dog than be bitten by him in contesting for the right. Even killing the dog would not cure the bite.

A. Lincoln

In this and like communities, public sentiment is everything. With public sentiment, nothing can fail; without it nothing can succeed.

A. Lincoln

Upon the subject of education, not presuming to dictate any plan or system respecting it, I can only say that I view it as the most important subject which we as a people can be engaged in.

I happen temporarily to occupy this big White House. I am living witness that any one of your children may look to come here as my father's child has.

A. Lincoln

*W*hat is conservatism? Is it not adherence to the old and tried, against the new and untried?

A. Lincoln

*W*ith malice toward none, with charity for all, with firmness in the right as God gives us to see the right, let us strive on to finish the work we are in; to bind up the nation's wounds; to care for him who shall have borne the battle, and for his widow, and his orphan—to do all which may achieve and cherish a just, and a lasting peace, among ourselves, and with all nations.

I have always thought that all men should be free; but if any should be slaves it should be first those who desire it for themselves, and secondly those who desire it for others. Whenever I hear anyone arguing for slavery I feel a strong impulse to see it tried on him personally.

A. Lincoln

*T*he true rule, in determining to embrace, or reject any thing, is not whether it have any evil in it; but whether it have more of evil, than of good. There are few things wholly evil, or wholly good. Almost every thing, especially of governmental policy, is an inseparable compound of the two; so that our best judgment of the preponderance between them is continually demanded.

*T*he dogmas of the quiet past, are inade-
quate to the stormy present. The occasion
is piled high with difficulty, and we must
rise with the occasion. As our case is new,
so we must think anew, and act anew. We
must disenthrall ourselves, and then we
shall save our country.

A. Lincoln

*W*e all declare for liberty; but in using
the same word we do not all mean the
same thing. With some the word liberty
may mean for each man to do as he pleases
with himself, and the product of his labor;
while with others the same word may
mean for some men to do as they please
with other men, and the product of other
men's labor.

*F*ourscore and seven years ago our fathers brought forth on this continent, a new nation, conceived in Liberty, and dedicated to the proposition that all men are created equal.

Now we are engaged in a great civil war, testing whether that nation or any nation so conceived and so dedicated, can long endure. We are met on a great battlefield of that war. We have come to dedicate a portion of that field as a final resting place for those who here gave their lives that that nation might live. It is altogether fitting and proper that we should do this.

But, in a larger sense, we cannot dedicate—we cannot consecrate—we cannot hallow—this ground. The brave men, living and dead, who struggled here, have consecrated it, far above our poor power to add or detract. The world will little note, nor long remember what we say here, but it can never forget what they did here. It is for us the living, rather, to be dedicated here to the unfinished work which they who fought here have thus far so nobly advanced. It is rather for us to be here dedicated to the great task remaining before us—that from these honored dead we take increased devotion to that cause for which they gave the last full measure of devotion—that we here highly resolve that these dead shall not have died in vain—that this nation, under God, shall have a new birth of freedom—and that government of the people, by the people, for the people, shall not perish from the earth.

A. Lincoln

If all do not join now to save the good old ship of the Union this voyage, nobody will have a chance to pilot her on another voyage.

*T*owering genius disdains a beaten path.
It seeks regions hitherto unexplored.

A.Lincoln

*I*f you would win a man to your cause, first
convince him that you are his sincere
friend. Therein is a drop of honey that
catches his heart, which, say what he will,
is the great high road to his reason, and
which, when once gained, you will find but
little trouble in convincing his judgment of
the justice of your cause, if indeed that
cause really be a just one.

A.Lincoln

*N*o man is good enough to govern
another man without that other's consent.

A.Lincoln

*T*he better part of one's life consists of his
friendships.

*I*n regard to this Great Book, I have but to say, it is the best gift God has given to man. All the good the Savior gave to the world was communicated through this book.

A. Lincoln

*H*is [Douglas's] explanations explanatory of explanations explained are interminable.

A. Lincoln

*Q*uarrel not at all. No man resolved to make the most of himself can spare time for personal contention. Still less can he afford to take all the consequences, including the vitiating of his temper and loss of self control.

I am rather inclined to silence, and whether that be wise or not, it is at least more unusual nowadays to find a man who can hold his tongue than to find one who cannot.

A. Lincoln

*T*he shepherd drives the wolf from the sheep's throat, for which the sheep thanks the shepherd as his liberator, while the wolf denounces him for the same act as the destroyer of liberty.

A. Lincoln

*I*t is the eternal struggle between these two principles—right and wrong—through-out the world. They are the two principles that have stood face to face from the beginning of time; and will ever continue to struggle.

I claim not to have controlled events, but confess plainly that events have controlled me.

A. Lincoln

I believe this Government cannot endure, permanently half slave and half free.

A. Lincoln

*A*nd by virtue of the power, and for the purpose aforesaid, I do order and declare that all persons held as slaves within said designated States, and parts of States, are, and henceforward shall be free; and that the Executive government of the United States, including the military and naval authorities thereof, will recognize and maintain the freedom of said persons.

*N*obody has ever expected me to be President. In my poor, lean, lank face nobody has ever seen that any cabbages were sprouting out.

A. Lincoln

*I*n great contests each party claims to act in accordance with the will of God. Both may be, and one must be wrong. God can not be for, and against the same thing at the same time.

A. Lincoln

*P*assion has helped us; but can do so no more. It will in future be our enemy. Reason, cold, calculating, unimpassioned reason, must furnish all the materials for our future support and defence.

I intend no modification of my oft-expressed personal wish that all men everywhere could be free.

A. Lincoln

That some should be rich, shows that others may become rich, and, hence, is just encouragement to industry and enterprise.

A. Lincoln

The demon of intemperance ever seems to have delighted in sucking the blood of genius and of generosity.

A. Lincoln

The man does not live who is more devoted to peace than I am. None who would do more to preserve it.

I am not bound to win, but I am bound to be true. I am not bound to succeed, but I am bound to live by the light that I have. I must stand with anybody that stands right, and stand with him while he is right, and part with him when he goes wrong.

A. Lincoln

T he probability that we may fail in the struggle ought not to deter us from the support of a cause we believe to be just.

A. Lincoln

E very man is said to have his peculiar ambition. Whether it be true or not, I can say, for one, that I have no other so great as that of being truly esteemed of my fellow men, by rendering myself worthy of their esteem.

$\mathcal{A}$ capacity and taste for reading gives access to whatever has already been discovered by others. It is the key, or one of the keys, to the already solved problems. And not only so, it gives a relish and facility for successfully pursuing the yet unsolved ones.

A. Lincoln

I believe it is an established maxim in morals that he who makes an assertion without knowing whether it is true or false, is guilty of falsehood; and the accidental truth of the assertion does not justify or excuse him.

A. Lincoln

$\mathcal{D}$ iscourage litigation. Persuade your neighbors to compromise whenever you can. Point out to them how the nominal winner is often a real loser—in fees, expenses, and waste of time. As a peace-maker the lawyer has a superior opportunity of being a good man. There will still be business enough.

I have been driven many times upon my knees by the overwhelming conviction that I had nowhere else to go. My own wisdom and that of all about me seemed insufficient for that day.

A. Lincoln

*T*here is no grievance that is a fit object of redress by mob law.

A. Lincoln

*I*f any personal description of me is thought desirable, it may be said, I am, in height, six feet, four inches, nearly; lean in flesh, weighing on an average one hundred and eighty pounds; dark complexion, with coarse black hair, and grey eyes—no other brands or marks recollected.

*I*n *giving* freedom to the *slave*, we *assure* freedom to the *free*—honorable alike in what we give, and what we preserve. We shall nobly save, or meanly lose, the last, best hope of earth.

A. Lincoln

I have never had a feeling politically that did not spring from the sentiments embodied in the Declaration of Independence.

A. Lincoln

*E*very man is proud of what he does well; and no man is proud of what he does not do well. With the former, his heart is in his work; and he will do twice as much of it with less fatigue. The latter performs a little imperfectly, looks at it in disgust, turns from it, and imagines himself exceedingly tired. The little he has done, comes to nothing, for want of finishing.

*C*ommon looking people are the best in the world: that is the reason the Lord makes so many of them.

A. Lincoln

*N*early all men can stand adversity, but if you want to test a man's character, give him power.

A. Lincoln

*A*s I would not be a slave, so I would not be a master. This expresses my idea of democracy. Whatever differs from this, to the extent of the difference, is no democracy.

*F*ellow citizens, we cannot escape history.

A. Lincoln

*N*either party expected for the war, the magnitude, or the duration, which it has already attained. Neither anticipated that the cause of the conflict might cease with, or even before, the conflict itself should cease. Each looked for an easier triumph, and a result less fundamental and astounding. Both read the same Bible, and pray to the same God; and each invokes His aid against the other. It may seem strange that any men should dare to ask a just God's assistance in wringing their bread from the sweat of other men's faces; but let us judge not, that we be not judged. The prayers of both could not be answered; that of neither has been answered fully. The Almighty has His own purposes.

*T*he way for a young man to rise, is to improve himself every way he can, never suspecting that any body wishes to hinder him.

A.Lincoln

*F*amiliarize yourself with the chains of bondage and you prepare your own limbs to wear them. Accustomed to trample on the rights of others, you have lost the genius of your own independence and become the fit subjects of the first cunning tyrant who rises among you.

A.Lincoln

I leave you, hoping that the lamp of liberty will burn in your bosoms until there shall no longer be a doubt that all men are created free and equal.

A. Lincoln